Eye Spy SEEK & FiND

ACTiViTY BOOK

JUPiTER KiDS

JUPITER KIDS
CHILDREN'S & KIDS FICTION

All Rights reserved. No part of this book may be reproduced or used in any way or form or by any means whether electronic or mechanical, this means that you cannot record or photocopy any material ideas or tips that are provided in this book.

Copyright 2016

S0-BYE-283

HELP ME FIND THIS!

HELP ME FIND THIS!

HELP ME FIND THIS!

HELP ME FIND THIS!

HELP ME FIND THIS!

HELP ME FIND THIS!

HELP ME FIND THIS!

HELP ME FIND THIS!

HELP ME FIND THIS!

HELP ME FIND THIS!

HELP ME FIND THIS!

HELP ME FIND THIS!

THE FUTURE IS NOW

HELP ME FIND THIS!

HELP ME FIND THIS!

HELP ME FIND THIS!

HELP ME FIND THIS!

HELP ME FIND THIS!

HELP ME FIND THIS!

HELP ME
FIND
THIS!

HELP ME
FIND
THIS!

HELP ME
FIND
THIS!

HELP ME FIND THIS!

HELP ME FIND THIS!

HELP ME FIND THIS!

HELP ME FIND THIS!

HELP ME FIND THIS!

HELP ME
FIND
THIS!

HELP ME
FIND
THIS!

THE FUTURE
IS NOW

HELP ME
FIND
THiS!

ANSWERS

Answer #3

Answer #4

Answer #5

Answer #6

Answer #7

HELP ME
FIND
THIS!

Answer #8

HELP ME
FIND
THIS!

Answer #9

Answer #10

Answer #11

Answer #12

Answer #13

Answer #14

Answer #15

HELP ME FIND THIS!

Answer #16

HELP ME FIND THIS!

Answer #17

Answer #18

Answer #19

HELP ME FIND THIS!

Answer #20

HELP ME FIND THIS!

Answer #21

Answer #22

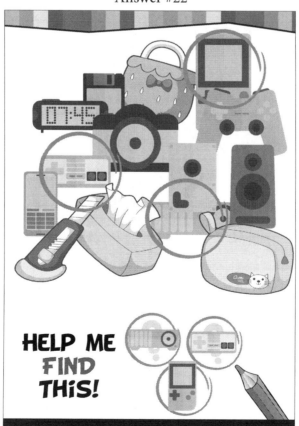

Answer #23

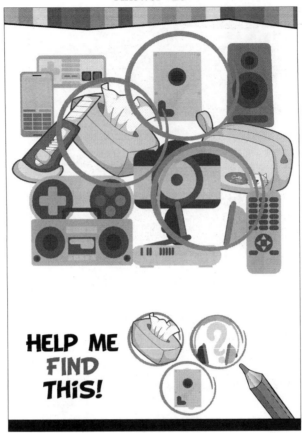

Answer #24

Answer #29

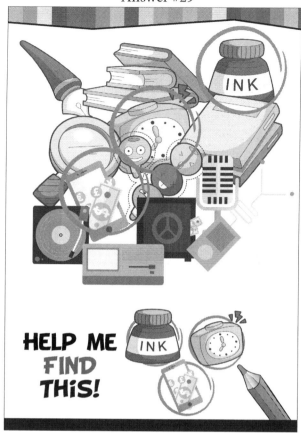

Answer #30

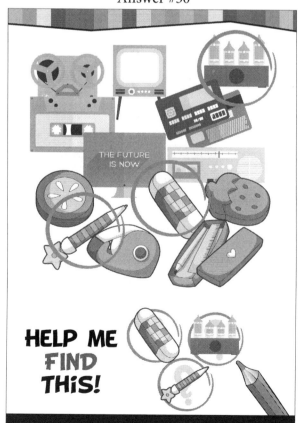

65585178R00029

Made in the USA
Lexington, KY
17 July 2017